Keto Desserts: 30 Healthy Keto Dessert Recipes

Everyday Easy Keto Desserts and Sugar Free Sweet Keto Diet Desserts

By Brendan Fawn

Legal & Disclaimer

The information contained in this book and its contents is not designed to replace or take the place of any form of medical or professional advice; and is not meant to replace the need for independent medical, financial, legal or other professional advice or services, as may be required. The content and information in this book has been provided for educational and entertainment purposes only.

The content and information contained in this book has been compiled from sources deemed reliable, and it is accurate to the best of the Author's knowledge, information and belief. However, the Author cannot guarantee its accuracy and validity and cannot be held liable for any errors and/or omissions. Further, changes are periodically made to this book as and when needed. Where appropriate and/or necessary, you must consult a professional (including but not limited to your doctor, attorney, financial advisor or such other professional advisor) before using any of the suggested remedies, techniques, or information in this book.

Upon using the contents and information contained in this book, you agree to hold harmless the Author from and against any damages, costs, and expenses, including any legal fees potentially resulting from the application of any of the information provided by this book. This disclaimer applies to any loss, damages or injury caused by the use and application, whether directly or indirectly, of any advice or information presented, whether for breach of contract, tort, negligence, personal injury, criminal intent, or under any other cause of action.

You agree to accept all risks of using the information presented in this book.

You agree that by continuing to read this book, where appropriate and/or necessary, you shall consult a professional (including but not limited to your doctor, attorney, or financial advisor or such other advisor as needed) before using any of the suggested remedies, techniques, or information in this book.

Table of Contents

1. Almond Pumpkin Pudding

2. Lemon Walnut Muffins

3. Chocolate Banana Muffins

4. White Chocolate Pecan Halves

5. Orange Walnut Cookies

6. Coconut Chocolate Truffles

7. Small Cherry Choco Muffins

8. Strawberries Chocolate Ice Cream

9. Chocolate Macadamia Nuts Cookies

10. 1-Carb Raspberry and Lemon Gummy Candies

11. Coconut Pudding

12. Strawberry Double Layer Cake

13. Cocoa Vanilla Soufflé

About This Cookbook

This cookbook contains delicious and sweet keto dessert recipes to help you start your ketogenic diet, lose weight, become healthier and boost your energy level.

Sweet keto desserts are the best solution for you if you want to eat something sweet, but still healthy. There is no need to deprive yourself of delicious sweet things if your goal is to lose weight or simply maintain the good condition of your body.

Enjoy puddings, chocolate muffins, walnut cookies, healthy strawberries ice cream, pancakes and much more. In this cookbook you will find a collection of 30 delicious sweet keto dessert recipes that will help you to work towards your health goals every day of the month.

Let's begin!

About the Keto Diet

The Basics of the Ketogenic Diet

More and more people in the United States and around the world are using the ketogenic diet. The latest studies have revealed that the keto diet helps you to reduce your health risk factors. Research shows a faster weight loss when participants go on a ketogenic or very low carbohydrate diet compared to patients on a more traditional low-fat diet, or even a Mediterranean diet (Campos, 2017). Keto diet helps to control cholesterol level, blood pressure level, heart diseases, diabetes, epilepsy, increases your energy level and more.

The keto diet is based on changing people's habits of eating high carbohydrate (carb) foods. Being on keto means that you will eat low carb, medium protein and high fat foods such as cheeses, cream, butter, all kinds of meats and fish, nuts, seeds, oils, berries, colorful fresh vegetables, greens, and such sweeteners as stevia or erythritol. You should also reduce the consumption of processed and chemically treated meals. The ketogenic diet contains mainly high fat foods (around 70%), but has very low carb meals and puts your body into a state called **ketosis**.

If you eat a lot of carbs, your body will produce a lot of glucose and insulin, which eventually may lead to prediabetes and type 2 diabetes.

- **Glucose** from carbohydrates is the main energy source for your body.

- **Insulin** hormone helps your body to use the glucose and enter cells.

> **"More than 100 million adults in the U.S. have diabetes or prediabetes."**

When you eliminate carb food and eat mainly low carb food, your body will start producing **ketones** from the breakdown of fats in your liver. Ketones will be used as the main source of energy by your body. The main goal of keto diet is to reach and maintain in this state called **ketosis**, which will give a lot of health benefits.

> **"Ketosis is a process that takes place in our bodies to help us survive when food intake is low."**

Why Go Keto?

The main and most visible advantage of being on keto that you will see after first weeks and even days is weight loss. A period of low carbohydrate keto diet may help to control hunger. That fact may improve fat oxidative metabolism and that will help to reduce your body weight (Paoli, 2014). When you are on a ketogenic diet, your body becomes efficient in burning fat as a main source of energy. When fat is used for fuel you will feel a more consistent energy flow in your body, moreover, you won't feel the highs and lows that you would normally feel when consuming high carb food, because of glucose levels spiking in your blood.

> **"Eating keto meals will allow you to feel more stable and less exhausted."**

In addition to these advantages, consuming keto dishes over a long period of time you will gain more benefits.

- Loss of weight and fat in particular parts of your body

- Blood sugar and insulin level control (preventing the risk of prediabetes and type 2 diabetes)

- Improved concentration, but also brain function

- Optimized blood pressure

- Normalized good and bad cholesterol levels

- Normalized hunger level

- Improved and increased energy level

Types of Ketogenic Diets

1) SKD – Standard Ketogenic Diet is the most popular diet. This type of keto diet means, that you will eat extremely low carb (around 5%), medium protein (around 20%) and high fat (around 75%) food.

2) High Protein Ketogenic Diet is the same as SKD but contains higher amounts of protein (around 35%), less fat (around 60%), and the same amount of carbs as SKD (5%).

3) CKD – Cyclical Ketogenic Diet is less strict than SKD because you can have "free keto days" and eat high carb dishes. For example, Mondays and Wednesdays are the days when you eat high carb food, and other days of the week are the ones you consume standard keto food.

4) TKD – Targeted Ketogenic Diet is a standard keto diet with the one exception of consuming carb food around your physical exercise or training.

KETO DIET Fats 70%, Protein 25%, Carbs 5%

Kitchen Utensils That You Will Need

To prepare the tasty and delicious sweet keto desserts, you will need to have the right tools in your kitchen. The following list of kitchen utensils will help you prepare your sweet keto desserts faster.

Food Scale

The food scale is the main and very important, because you can use it to measure any solid or liquid food, and it will always indicate the quantity of ingredients that you need for preparing the sweet ketogenic desserts. Moreover, you can use your food scale in combination with a diet app, and get all the data you need to eat more intelligently and reach your keto diet goals more efficiently.

"Use the food scale with a diet app to reach your keto diet goals faster."

Food Processor or Blender

Having a food processor or blender is critical for preparing keto desserts because it will help you to process, grind, pulse, and blend eggs, stevia, berries, cream, nuts etc.

Electric Hand Mixer

Using an electric hand mixer will save your time and energy, especially when you are preparing keto desserts where you need to combine various ingredients such as pulsed berries or nuts with eggs, erythritol, cream or baking powder.

Paper Muffin Cups or Candy Cups

Paper muffin cups, candy cups, silicone molds, baking cups, baking trays or sheets are crucial when preparing sweet keto desserts, because often you need to bake, to store, to freeze all your sweet mixtures.

The following chapters contain delicious sweet keto dessert recipes that will sweeten your keto diet days and will have your taste buds come to life!

1. Almond Pumpkin Pudding

Pumpkin is a real miracle, because it is a vegetable full of minerals and vitamins, such as B1, B6, PP and others that are responsible for the various key processes in our bodies. It contains a lot of carotenes - vitamin A - that is four and a half times higher in pumpkin than in carrots! Pumpkin is also very delicious! If you prepare the pudding from the pumpkin adding coconut cream and fresh lemon juice you will feel the airiness and tenderness in your mouth while tasting it and this dish will become your favorite ketogenic dessert.

Prep Time: 10 min. | Cooking Time: 10 min. | Servings: 10

Ingredients:

- 10 oz pumpkin puree

- 5 oz coconut cream

- 5 oz coconut oil

- 1 tablespoon pumpkin-pie spice

- 3 tbsp. powdered erythritol

- 4 oz almonds

- 3/4 teaspoon ginger

Instructions:

1. Melt the coconut cream, coconut oil, pumpkin puree, pumpkin-pie spice, erythritol, ginger on medium heat, stirring for around 10 minutes.

2. Pour the mixture into the silicone molds and press the almond inside each pudding mold.

3. Freeze the pudding for at least 1 hour and then you are free to serve it.

Tip: *You can squeeze fresh lemon juice and pour over the pudding.*

Nutrients per serving:

Net Carbs: 4g; Total Fat: 16g; Protein: 6g; Calories: 154

2. Lemon Walnut Muffins

Lemon gives these muffins unforgettable freshness! What is more they are rich in vitamins due to walnuts. You can chat for hours with your friends, eating those muffins. Your friends they will love them!

Prep Time: 15 min. | Cooking Time: 25 min. | Servings: 7

Ingredients:

- 7 oz walnuts, ground
- 2 tsp. lemon zest, minced
- 2 eggs
- 4 oz coconut butter
- 20 drops of stevia
- 2 tbsp. baking powder
- cinnamon
- sugar-free spray cream

Instructions:

1. Place the coconut butter and stevia into a food processor and blend.

2. Then, add in the lemon zest, walnuts, eggs, baking powder, and cinnamon and blend, using a food processor until they have a smooth and creamy consistency.

3. Spoon the mixture into the silicone molds, muffin or baking cups and bake for 25 minutes at 320°-330°Fahrenheit. Then cool, and serve with the spray cream on top.

Nutrients per serving:

Net Carbs: 2.5g; Total Fat: 24g; Protein: 11g; Calories: 213

3. Chocolate Banana Muffins

Banana extract will add the new accent to these chocolate muffins that have a very tender and pleasant soft taste. Your relatives and family will always ask for more!

Prep Time: 25 min. | Cooking Time: 40 min. | Servings: 8

Ingredients:

- 5 oz unsweetened chocolate
- 8 oz almond butter
- 8 oz cocoa powder
- 3 eggs
- 20 drops of stevia
- 1 tbsp. erythritol
- 1 tbsp. banana extract
- 3 tbsp. baking powder
- vanilla
- sea salt

Instructions:

1. Place the almond butter and stevia into a food processor and blend.

2. Blend the mixture with the eggs, cocoa powder, banana extract, baking powder, vanilla, and salt, using a food processor until they have a smooth and creamy consistency.

3. Spoon the mixture into the silicone molds or muffin cups and bake for 30 minutes at 320°-330° Fahrenheit.

4. Melt the unsweetened chocolate on low heat for around 10 minutes, stirring all the time.

5. Cool the chocolate and slowly pour it over the muffins.

6. The muffins should be placed in the fridge for 1 hour.

Nutrients per serving:

Net Carbs: 2.6g; Total Fat: 25g; Protein: 13g; Calories: 247

4. White Chocolate Pecan Halves

Just few simple steps and you will taste these mouthwatering choco pecan halves. Crunchy keto snacks with healthy fats and sweet flavors are worth to try them!

Prep Time: 20 min. | Cooking Time: 10 min. | Servings: 10

Ingredients:

- 10 oz pecan halves
- 10 caramel sugar free candies
- 2 oz cocoa butter
- 3 tablespoons erythritol
- cinnamon

Instructions:

1. Preheat the oven to 280°- 300° Fahrenheit.

2. Add the candies onto each pecan halve and bake until the candies are slightly melted.

3. Melt together the cocoa butter, erythritol and cinnamon for 10 minutes until smooth and creamy consistency.

4. Spoon the mixture onto each pecan halve and place in the fridge for around 2 hours.

Nutrients per serving:

Net Carbs: 1.4g; Total Fat: 8.9g; Protein: 2g; Calories: 123

5. Orange Walnut Cookies

I love these sugar-free orange cookies and I think you will love them too! Crispy and delicious!

Prep Time: 15 min. | Cooking Time: 50 min. | Servings: 10

Ingredients:

- 8 oz walnut halves
- 3 tbsp. orange zest, minced
- 1 egg
- 20 drops of stevia
- shredded coconut
- cinnamon

Instructions:

1. Toast the walnut halves in the oven for 10 minutes until lightly browned and blend them using a food processor.

2. Add all the ingredients into a food processor and blend until they have a smooth consistency.

3. Form 10 balls out of the mixture, flatten slightly, add the shredded coconut on top, and bake for 40 minutes at 300° - 320°Fahrenheit.

Nutrients per serving:

Net Carbs: 4g; Total Fat: 17g; Protein: 7g; Calories: 137

6. Coconut Chocolate Truffles

These chocolate truffles will please all your guests! Use this recipe when you want to impress your guests!

Prep Time: 20 min. | Cooking Time: 10 min. | Servings: 10

Ingredients:

- 4 oz unsweetened chocolate

- 4 oz heavy cream

- 3 oz cocoa powder

- 4 oz shredded coconut

- 2 oz unsalted butter

- 4 oz powdered erythritol

- vanilla

Instructions:

1. Heat the heavy cream and the unsweetened chocolate in a double boiler for 10 minutes until melted.

2. Add all the remaining ingredients except for the shredded coconut into a food processor and blend

until they have a smooth consistency, and place in the fridge for 1 hour.

3. Form 10 balls out of the mixture and roll them in the shredded coconut and place in the fridge for around 2 hours, then enjoy!

<u>**Tip:**</u> *Form the balls with lightly oiled hands.*

Nutrients per serving:

Net Carbs: 3g; Total Fat: 21g; Protein: 10g; Calories: 179

7. Small Cherry Choco Muffins

Sugar-free keto friendly and small in size muffins could be delicious dessert for you guests! Fresh cherries on top will and charm to this mouthwatering dessert.

Prep Time: 15 min. | Cooking Time: 20 min. | Servings: 15

Ingredients:

- 2 oz fresh cherries
- 4 oz sugar free cherry syrup
- 2 eggs
- 4 oz coconut butter
- 5 oz cocoa powder
- 2 tbsp. baking powder
- 20 drops of stevia

Instructions:

1. Blend together the coconut butter and stevia using a food processor.
2. Then, add in the cherry syrup, eggs, cocoa powder and baking powder.

3. Pour the mixture into each small muffin cup, candy cup or silicone candy mold, place the cherry on top of each muffin, and bake for 15-20 minutes at 320°-330°Fahrenheit.

Nutrients per serving:

Net Carbs: 2.5g; Total Fat: 23g; Protein: 4.9g; Calories: 269

8. Strawberries Chocolate Ice Cream

This sugar-free, low-carb and artificial coloring-free ice cream is paleo and keto friendly! The light red color comes from strawberries!

Prep Time: 25 min. | Cooking Time: 0 min. | Servings: 10

Preparation time: 25 minutes

Cooking time: 0 minutes

Servings: 10

Ingredients:

- 5 oz strawberries
- 5 oz unsweetened chocolate chips
- 23 oz unsweetened coconut milk
- 25 drops of liquid stevia
- vanilla

Instructions:

1. Blend the coconut milk, strawberries, stevia, and vanilla using a food processor.

2. Combine the mixture with the unsweetened chocolate chips in a mixing bowl, mashing with a fork.

3. Spoon the mixture into the ice cream maker and process for 1 hour or according to manufacturer's instructions.

4. Spoon the strawberries mixture into the silicone molds or an ice tray and freeze for overnight.

Nutrients per serving:

Net Carbs: 3g; Total Fat: 17g; Protein: 5g; Calories: 173

9. Chocolate Macadamia Nuts Cookies

Sweet and healthy! Crispy macadamia nuts cookies. Try something you will not forget!

Prep Time: 20 min. | Cooking Time: 40 min. | Servings: 10

Ingredients:

- 5 oz macadamia nuts, ground
- 8 oz heavy cream
- 4 tbsp. granular erythritol
- 2 oz shredded coconut
- 2 tablespoons cocoa powder
- 4 oz unsweetened chocolate chips
- vanilla

Instructions:

1. Melt the heavy cream and erythritol on medium heat, stirring for around 10 minutes.
2. Combine the heavy cream mixture and all the remaining ingredients in a mixing bowl, using a hand mixer.

3. Spoon the sweet dough onto the baking sheet and bake for about 30 minutes at 320°- 330°Fahrenheit, then cool, and serve.

Nutrients per serving:

Net Carbs: 6g; Total Fat: 26g; Protein: 7.8g; Calories: 279

10. 1-Carb Raspberry and Lemon Gummy Candies

Prepare these raspberry and lemon gummy candies and play with gelatin proportions that will give you a lot of fun! You can use other type of berries as well.

Prep Time: 20 min. | Cooking Time: 10 min. | Servings: 12

Ingredients:

- 2 packets unflavored gelatin

- 5 oz raspberries

- 4 tbsp. lemon zest, minced

- 1 packet (3 oz) sugar-free raspberries gelatin dessert (Jell-O)

- 1 packet (3 oz) sugar-free lemon gelatin dessert (Jell-O)

- 10 drops of stevia

Instructions:

1. Pour the water into the gelatin and Jell-O, and heat gently for 10 minutes, stirring, warming up almost to a boil, until dissolved.

2. Add the raspberries, stevia and pour the mixture into the silicone molds, and place in the fridge overnight.

3. Make the same with the lemon zest and lemon Jell-O.

Tip: *Let the gelatin mixture cool, before placing in the fridge.*

Nutrients per serving:

Net Carbs: 1g; Total Fat: 2g; Protein: 1.5g; Calories: 95

11. Coconut Pudding

Thought you will never like the coconut in your pudding? Well, you will change your mind if you try this exotic coconut taste pudding. Coconut will make this pudding more delicious. Feel like you're on Caribbean island for a second!

Prep Time: 20 min. | Cooking Time: 25 min. | Servings: 10

Ingredients:

- 8 oz shredded coconut
- 4 oz unsweetened creamed coconut milk
- 4 oz heavy cream
- 1 egg yolk
- 20 drops of stevia
- 1 tsp. xanthan gum

Instructions:

1. Melt together the heavy cream, creamed coconut milk, egg yolk and stevia in a double boiler for 10 minutes until they have a smooth and creamy consistency.

2. Add the xanthan gum and keep stirring for around 15 minutes until thickened.

3. Add in the shredded coconut and pour the mixture into glasses and place in the fridge for around 5 hours.

<u>**Tip:**</u> *Stevia drops could be substituted by powdered erythritol.*

Nutrients per serving:

Net Carbs: 4g; Total Fat: 32g; Protein: 5g; Calories: 251

12.   Strawberry Double Layer Cake

This strawberry double layer cake has unusual structure, but is easy and fast to prepare, moreover thanks to strawberry gelatin it is moist. Family favorite!

Prep Time: 25 min. | Cooking Time: 30 min. | Servings: 10

Ingredients:

- 4 oz almonds
- 4 oz strawberries
- 2 tbsp. unsalted butter
- 1 packet (3 oz) sugar-free strawberry gelatin dessert
- 9 oz cream cheese
- vanilla

Instructions:

1. Melt the unsalted butter in a skillet and add the vanilla.
2. Blend the almonds with the melted butter and strawberries using a food processor, but don't overblend.

3. Spoon the mixture into the silicone molds or muffin cups and bake for 20 minutes at 320°-330°Fahrenheit and then cool the crust for 20 minutes.

4. Pour the water into the strawberry gelatin dessert, and heat gently for 10 minutes, stirring, warming up almost to a boil, until dissolved.

5. Then, add cream cheese and whisk until smooth and creamy consistency.

6. Pour the gelatin mixture over baked crusts and place in the fridge overnight.

Nutrients per serving:

Net Carbs: 5g; Total Fat: 35g; Protein: 10g; Calories: 254

13.   Cocoa Vanilla Soufflé

The sweet aroma of vanilla pairs nicely with the bitter taste of cocoa. Light soufflé will add delicious taste to your keto breakfast.

Prep Time: 20 min. | Cooking Time: 30 min. | Servings: 6

Ingredients:

- 10 oz cocoa powder

- 3 eggs

- 4 oz unsalted butter

- 3 tbsp. powdered erythritol

- 3 tsp. baking powder

- frozen strawberries

- vanilla

Instructions:

1. Melt the unsalted butter in a skillet for 10 minutes and add the vanilla.

2. Beat the egg whites and egg yolks separately using a hand mixer.

3. Combine egg yolks with the melted butter, erythritol, baking powder and cocoa powder.

4. Pour the egg whites into egg yolks mixture and mix until they have a smooth and creamy consistency.

5. Pour the mixture into each muffin cup, candy cup or silicone mold and bake for 20 minutes at 320°-330°Fahrenheit, add frozen strawberry on top and serve immediately, because they will start to melt right away.

Tip: *Egg whites and egg yolks should be beaten separately; it is very important step to remember.*

Nutrients per serving:

Net Carbs: 2g; Total Fat: 13g; Protein: 5g; Calories: 98

14.   Chocolate Almond Square Fudge

Smooth, light, creamy and super fudgy! Chocolate and almonds are very healthy and these choco squares are full of creamy, bitter chocolate taste!

Prep Time: 25 min. | Cooking Time: 20 min. | Servings: 15

Ingredients:

- 8 oz cream cheese
- 10 tbsp. coconut oil
- 10 oz cocoa powder
- 10 drops of stevia
- 4 tablespoons monk fruit sweetener
- 2 oz unsweetened dark chocolate
- 4 oz almonds, ground
- vanilla

Instructions:

1. Melt the cream cheese, coconut oil, cocoa powder, stevia, monk fruit sweetener, and chocolate on medium heat, stirring for around 20 minutes until they have a creamy and smooth consistency.

2. Spoon the sweet mixture into silicone pan and spread it with a spatula.

3. Sprinkle with the almonds on top and place in the fridge for at least 4 hours, then cut into 15 squares and serve.

Tip: *In step 1 you can beat the sweet mixture with an electric hand mixer to make it extra creamy.*

Nutrients per serving:

Net Carbs: 4g; Total Fat: 24g; Protein: 6g; Calories: 213

15. Strawberry Vanilla Mousse

Super delicious light mousse! Strawberries give unforgettable aroma and creamy texture without adding extra carbs or fats!

Prep Time: 25 min. | Cooking Time: 5 min. | Servings: 10

Ingredients:

- 2 oz fresh or frozen strawberries
- 4 oz unsalted butter
- 4 oz cream cheese
- 4 tablespoons monk fruit sweetener
- vanilla

Instructions:

1. Defrost the frozen strawberries in your microwave if frozen.

2. Melt the unsalted butter in a pan over low heat for a few minutes until golden brown.

3. Beat together the strawberries, unsalted butter, cream cheese, monk fruit sweetener and vanilla in a mixing bowl, until they have a smooth and creamy consistency, using an electric hand mixer.

4. Spoon the strawberry mixture into the jars and freeze for around 20 minutes serving with a strawberry on top.

Nutrients per serving:

Net Carbs: 5g; Total Fat: 32g; Protein: 7g; Calories: 226

16. Dark Chocolate Cake

Chocolate has a lot of calories in it. Moreover, dark chocolate contains a lot of vital vitamins that are crucial for our body, such as magnesium, iron, and vitamin B12. So this dark chocolate cake is not only very tasty, but also is very healthy!

Prep Time: 20 min. | Cooking Time: 35 min. | Servings: 4

Ingredients:

- 4 oz unsweetened dark chocolate
- 8 oz almond flour
- 4 eggs
- 4 oz coconut oil
- 4 oz cocoa powder
- 8 tbsp. granular erythritol
- 10 drops of stevia
- 4 oz unsweetened chocolate chips
- cinnamon

Instructions:

1. Combine the almond flour with coconut oil, eggs, erythritol, cocoa powder, stevia, chocolate chips, and cinnamon in a mixing bowl, mashing with a fork until smooth.

2. Spoon the mixture into the silicone molds and bake for 20 minutes at 320°- 330°Fahrenheit, and then serve.

3. Melt the dark chocolate on a low heat, stirring for around 15 minutes and then slowly pour the melted chocolate over the cakes.

Nutrients per serving:

Net Carbs: 5g; Total Fat: 39g; Protein: 15g; Calories: 295

17.   Sweet Raspberries Pancakes

Very light and creamy pancakes with fresh raspberries will remind you summer days! Enjoy these keto friendly raspberries pancakes alone or with your friends and family.

Prep Time: 25 min. | Cooking Time: 12 min. | Servings: 12

Ingredients:

- 4 oz fresh raspberries
- 4 oz eggs, separated
- 5 oz cream cheese
- 2 tbsp. baking powder
- 20 drops of stevia
- sugar-free raspberry syrup
- vanilla

Instructions:

1. Place the raspberries and stevia into a food processor and blend until smooth.

2. Beat the egg whites using an electric hand mixer and then add the baking powder.

3. Beat the egg yolks, cream cheese, vanilla and raspberries mixture using an electric hand mixer and mix until they have a smooth and creamy consistency, then carefully combine with the egg whites.

4. Add the mixture into a frying pan and fry on a low heat for around 5-8 minutes, then flip and cook for 2-4 minutes and serve with sugar-free raspberry syrup on top.

Tip: *You can use the unsalted butter instead of the oil to fry the pancakes; this step will make them more delicious and tasty.*

Nutrients per serving:

Net Carbs: 4g; Total Fat: 19g; Protein: 8g; Calories: 189

18.   Peanut Coconut Fudge Squares

These peanut squares have a lot of healthy calories and fats! They are perfect for keto diet, as well as for your children!

Prep Time: 25 min. | Cooking Time: 20 min. | Servings: 15

Ingredients:

- 4 oz raw or roasted peanuts
- 10 oz almond butter
- 10 oz cocoa powder
- 4 eggs
- 5 oz shredded coconut
- 10 tbsp. powdered erythritol
- 10 drops of stevia
- 2 tsp. baking powder
- vanilla
- sugar-free chocolate syrup

Instructions:

1. Place the shredded coconut, almond butter, erythritol, vanilla and stevia into a food processor and blend until smooth.

2. Combine the sweet mixture with the eggs, peanuts, cocoa powder and baking powder.

3. Spoon the sweet mixture into the silicone baking pan, then spread and smooth the top of the mixture with a spatula.

4. Bake the mixture for 20 minutes at 320°-330°Fahrenheit. Then cool, cut into squares and serve with the sugar-free chocolate syrup on top.

Nutrients per serving:

Net Carbs: 5g; Total Fat: 16g; Protein: 9g; Calories: 149

19.   Crème Glacée

Crème glacée is the French phrase for ice cream. Taste delicious cocoa and vanilla ice cream and feel like you're in romantic Paris for a second!

Prep Time: 25 min. | Cooking Time: 10 min. | Servings: 8

Ingredients:

- 15 oz heavy cream
- 5 egg yolks
- 5 oz cocoa powder
- 15 drops of stevia
- 4 oz powdered erythritol
- shredded coconut
- vanilla

Instructions:

1. Place the heavy cream, cocoa powder, shredded coconut, stevia, erythritol and vanilla into a pot and heat gently for 10 minutes, stirring, warming up until dissolved.

2. Whisk the egg yolks and slowly pour the sweet heavy cream mixture, stirring all the time.

3. Pour the egg yolks mixture into the pot and heat gently for 10 minutes, stirring, warming up and then cool.

4. Spoon the mixture into the ice cream maker and process for 1 hour or according to manufacturer's instructions and freeze for at least 3 hours.

Nutrients per serving:

Net Carbs: 6g; Total Fat: 37g; Protein: 8g; Calories: 340

20. Tasty Orange Bars

Light and fresh orange aroma and taste! Your guests and friends will be happy after these magnificent and tasty orange bars! Finish them off with orange slices and pour with orange juice.

Prep Time: 20 min. | Cooking Time: 50 min. | Servings: 10

Ingredients:

- 4 tbsp. orange zest, minced

- 8 oz unsalted butter

- 10 oz almond flour

- 8 oz powdered erythritol

- 4 eggs

- 10 drops of stevia

- 4 oranges or kumquats

- vanilla

Instructions:

1. Melt the unsalted butter on medium heat for around 5 minutes, stirring all the time.

2. Combine the unsalted butter, 7 oz of the almond flour, vanilla and 6 oz of the powdered erythritol in a mixing bowl, mashing with a fork until smooth.

3. Spoon the mixture into the baking tray and bake for 20 minutes at 320°- 330°Fahrenheit.

4. Now let's start the filling by combining orange zest, freshly squeezed orange juice, eggs, remaining erythritol and almond flour.

5. Beat together the filling mixture, in a mixing bowl, using an electric hand mixer.

6. Then, pour the orange filling mixture onto the cooled almond crust and bake for 25 minutes at 320°- 330°Fahrenheit. Then, cool and serve with orange slices and some orange juice on top.

Nutrients per serving:

Net Carbs: 4.1g; Total Fat: 28g; Protein: 8g; Calories: 263

21. Twin Choco-Blueberry Mousse

Two chocolate types and few sweet, delicious layers are always better and tastier than one! Pour this twin choco-blueberry mousse into the glasses and enjoy its smoothness and lightness! Very fast to prepare!

Prep Time: 15 min. | Cooking Time: 0 min. | Servings: 6

Ingredients:

- 5 oz blueberries
- 8 oz heavy cream
- 5 oz cream cheese
- 5 oz powdered erythritol
- 4 oz cocoa powder
- sugar-free dark chocolate

Instructions:

1. Smash the blueberries using a blender and melt the chocolate on a low heat, stirring and adding 4 oz of the heavy cream.

2. Beat the cream cheese with erythritol using an electric hand mixer and combine with the cocoa

powder. Then, blend until they have a smooth and creamy consistency.

3. Beat the remaining heavy cream until whipped and creamy consistency and pour all the ingredients into the glasses in layers: chocolate, blueberries mixture, cocoa cream cheese and heavy cream, adding blueberries on top.

Nutrients per serving:

Net Carbs: 4.7g; Total Fat: 42g; Protein: 7g; Calories: 328

22.   Lemon Taste Crème Brûlée

Impress your friends and family with this lemon taste delicious lemon crème brûlée. Lemon aroma will add freshness to this classic keto dessert.

Prep Time: 30 min. | Cooking Time: 55 min. | Servings: 10

Ingredients:

- 3 tbsp. lemon zest, minced
- 15 oz heavy cream
- 4 egg yolks
- 4 oz granular erythritol
- 10 drops of liquid stevia
- vanilla
- sugar-free chocolate, grated

Instructions:

1. Combine the heavy cream with the erythritol and melt on a low heat, stirring for around 15 minutes until they have a creamy and smooth consistency.

2. Beat the egg yolks with the lemon zest, vanilla and stevia using an electric hand mixer, adding heavy cream, whisking until the creamy consistency.

3. Pour the mixture into the muffin tins or ramekins and place in a baking tray with the hot water reaching half the ramekins sides, and bake for 40 minutes at 300°- 310°Fahrenheit.

4. Sprinkle with grated chocolate, when it is hot, then cool the lemon crème brûlée for at least 4 hours, and then you are free to serve it.

Nutrients per serving:

Net Carbs: 4.5g; Total Fat: 45g; Protein: 8g; Calories: 387

23.   Chocolate Walnuts Clusters

No baking required this time! Crispy chocolate, walnuts and hazelnuts clusters would be a good substitute for candies and sugary sweets! Your kids will adore these healthy keto clusters!

Prep Time: 20 min. | Cooking Time: 20 min. | Servings: 10

Ingredients:

- 5 oz heavy cream

- 2 oz sugar-free dark chocolate

- 4 oz hazelnuts, ground

- 10 walnut halves

- 15 drops of stevia

Instructions:

1. Combine the heavy cream with the stevia, hazelnuts and chocolate and melt on a low heat, stirring for around 20 minutes until they have a creamy and smooth consistency.

2. Place the walnut halves on a parchment paper and spoon the mixture onto each walnut halve and place in the fridge for at least 4 hours, then serve.

Tip: *You can toast the walnut halves and hazelnuts in the oven for 10 minutes until lightly browned and crispy.*

Nutrients per serving:

Net Carbs: 1.9g; Total Fat: 13g; Protein: 2g; Calories: 99

24.   Hazelnut Coconut Cake

Sugar-free and tasty hazelnut cake is simple and fast to prepare. Light, healthy and sweet! Your kids will love this dessert for sure!

Prep Time: 20 min. | Cooking Time: 60 min. | Servings: 10

Ingredients:

- 20 oz hazelnuts, ground

- 20 oz sugar-free coconut milk

- 5 eggs

- 15 oz shredded coconut

- 8 oz powdered erythritol

- vanilla

- sugar-free spray cream

Instructions:

1. Combine coconut milk with erythritol and melt on a low heat, stirring for around 10 minutes until they have a smooth consistency.

2. Then, combine the mixture with the eggs, and all the remaining ingredients in a mixing bowl, and

beat using a hand mixer until they have a smooth and creamy consistency.

3. Spoon the sweet dough into the oiled baking tray and bake for about 50 minutes at 330°-340°Fahrenheit, then cool, cut and serve with the spray cream on top.

Nutrients per serving:

Net Carbs: 6g; Total Fat: 38g; Protein: 7g; Calories: 315

25.   Peanut Butter Choco Almond Cups

Peanut butter cookies could be sugar-free, but still sweet, and what is more extremely healthy! Try them and you will fall in love with them for the rest of your life!

Prep Time: 30 min. | Cooking Time: 10 min. | Servings: 10

Ingredients:

- 10 oz peanut butter
- 6 oz almonds
- 6 oz unsweetened dark chocolate
- 5 tbsp. coconut oil
- 8 tbsp. powdered erythritol
- 3 tbsp. monk fruit sweetener

Instructions:

1. Melt together the chocolate and coconut oil with monk fruit sweetener and 6 tbsp. of erythritol in a double boiler for 10 minutes until they have a smooth and creamy consistency.

2. Spoon the mixture into the silicone molds and press few almonds inside each chocolate mold.

3. Melt the peanut butter in the microwave and combine it with the remaining erythritol, stir well.

4. Spoon the peanut butter mixture into the silicone molds with the chocolate and then place in the fridge for around 2 hours and serve.

Nutrients per serving:

Net Carbs: 4.9g; Total Fat: 32g; Protein: 9g; Calories: 365

26. Dreams Come True Cheesecake

Forget about all your problems, tasting this light and soft cheesecake. Delicious, summer sweet taste that will have your taste buds coming to life!

Prep Time: 15 min. | Cooking Time: 35 min. | Servings: 4

Ingredients:

- fresh raspberries
- fresh blueberries
- 1 packet gelatin
- 4 oz sugar-free raspberries syrup
- 12 oz cream cheese
- 2 eggs
- 3 oz coconut oil
- 20 drops of stevia
- 4 tbsp. granular erythritol
- vanilla

Instructions:

1. Pour the water into the gelatin and heat gently, stirring, warming up almost to a boil, until dissolved, and then add raspberries syrup and cool.

2. Beat the cream cheese with the stevia and erythritol using an electric hand mixer until they have a smooth and creamy consistency.

3. Beat the eggs in a mixing bowl, mashing with a fork until whipped and smooth consistency, adding the cream cheese mixture.

4. Fill the baking tray with the mixture and bake for 35 minutes at 320°- 330°Fahrenheit, then pour the raspberries gelatin on top and refrigerate for overnight, cut into pieces and serve with the fresh raspberries and blueberries.

Nutrients per serving:

Net Carbs: 3.2g; Total Fat: 15g; Protein: 6g; Calories: 156

27.   Almond Coconut Cream Pie

Almond coconut cream pie is the delicious and tasty keto dessert for a romantic dinner. You will always stay in shape after this sweet keto pie!

Prep Time: 25 min. | Cooking Time: 20 min. | Servings: 10

Ingredients:

- 8 oz shredded coconut
- 5 oz almond, ground
- 15 oz heavy cream
- 6 oz coconut oil
- 10 drops of stevia
- 5 oz powdered erythritol
- vanilla

Instructions:

1. Beat the coconut oil with the 5 oz of erythritol and stevia in a mixing bowl, using a hand mixer.

2. Spoon the mixture into the baking tray and bake for 20 minutes at 330°- 340°Fahrenheit.

3. Melt the heavy cream on low heat, stirring for around 10 minutes, and then add almonds and remaining erythritol.

4. Pour the cream mixture onto the cooled coconut crust and sprinkle with the shredded coconut, then refrigerate for overnight and serve.

Nutrients per serving:

Net Carbs: 5g; Total Fat: 45g; Protein: 7g; Calories: 395

28. Exotic Taste Cupcakes

Fast and simple, these cupcakes are fast to make and have the exotic coconut taste. If you prepare the cupcakes adding the shredded coconut and lemon zest you will feel the airiness and tenderness in your mouth while tasting them and these exotic taste cupcakes will become your favorite.

Prep Time: 30 min. | Cooking Time: 40 min. | Servings: 8

Ingredients:

- 4 eggs

- 3 tbsp. lemon zest, minced

- 10 oz shredded coconut

- 8 oz coconut butter

- 7 oz dark chocolate

- 3 oz cocoa powder

- 4 tbsp. baking powder

- 20 drops of stevia

Instructions:

1. Melt the dark chocolate in your microwave and combine it with the stevia, coconut butter, lemon zest, shredded coconut and cocoa powder.

2. Beat the eggs until whipped, using an electric hand mixer and then add the baking powder.

3. Combine the chocolate mixture with the half of the eggs mixture and pour into the baking cups, then add the remaining eggs mixture on top and bake for 40 minutes at 310°- 320°Fahrenheit, then cool and serve.

Nutrients per serving:

Net Carbs: 2.2g; Total Fat: 15g; Protein: 6g; Calories: 135

29.   Delicious Hazelnut Cream

Are you on keto diet and want to eat something sweet, but standard hazelnut Nutella cream has a lot of sugars? No problem, you can use our recipe, if you don't want to consume a lot of unhealthy sugars! It will be the best breakfast recipe for your kids as well!

Prep Time: 30 min. | Cooking Time: 10 min. | Servings: 10 oz

Ingredients:

- 15 oz hazelnuts, roasted
- 5 oz cocoa powder
- 4 oz coconut oil
- 4 oz sugar-free almond milk
- 4 tablespoons monk fruit sweetener
- 5 oz powdered erythritol
- vanilla

Instructions:

1. Roast the hazelnuts in the oven for 10 minutes until lightly browned and crispy, and then blend using a food processor.

2. Add the coconut oil, cocoa powder, erythritol, monk fruit sweetener, vanilla and pulse up to a homogeneous mass.

3. Add the almond milk and blend until smooth and creamy consistency, then keep in the fridge for at least 5 hours.

Nutrients per serving:

Net Carbs: 4g; Total Fat: 19g, Protein: 7g; Calories: 193

30. Cashew Chocolate Muffins

Healthy sugar-free muffins are sweet enough for ketogenic dessert, but full of fats and proteins. Enjoy them with a cup of hot cocoa or coffe!

Prep Time: 30 min. | Cooking Time: 50 min. | Servings: 10

Ingredients:

- 1 cup of cashews
- 5 oz unsweetened chocolate
- 1 egg
- 1 cup flour
- 8 oz unsalted butter
- 1 tablespoon cream cheese
- 25 drops of stevia
- vanilla

Instructions:

1. Preheat the oven to 300°-320°Fahrenheit.
2. Toast the cashews in the oven for 10 minutes and then grind them using a blender.

3. Blend the cashews and all the remaining ingredients except for the white chocolate in a mixing bowl, using a hand mixer.

4. Make the crumbly dough, spoon the mixture into the silicone molds or baking cups and bake for 40 minutes at 300°- 320°Fahrenheit.

5. Melt the chocolate on low heat for around 10 minutes, stirring all the time.

6. Cool the chocolate and slowly pour it over the muffins.

7. Cool the cashew muffins for around 2 hours and then you are free to serve them.

Nutrients per serving:

Net Carbs: 7.5g; Total Fat: 28g; Protein: 12g; Calories: 261

Conclusion

Thank you for using this keto diet cookbook and preparing the sweet keto desserts.

If you are new in the field of sweet keto desserts, this cookbook will help you to start your sweet keto journey. Hope that you enjoyed the experimenting and preparing these keto pancakes, muffins, pies and other sweet keto desserts as I did!

If you've enjoyed this book, I'd greatly appreciate if you could leave an honest review on Amazon.

Reviews are very important to us authors, and it only takes a minute for you to post.

Your direct feedback could be used to help other readers to discover the advantages on going keto!

If you have anything you want me to know, any questions, suggestions or feedback, please don't hesitate to contact me: books777@gmx.com

If you have success story, please send it to me! I'm always happy to hear about my reader's success!

Thank you again and I hope you have enjoyed keto desserts cookbook.

Bibliography

Campos, M. (2017). *Ketogenic diet: Is the ultimate low-carb diet good for you?* Retrieved from Harvard Health Publishing: https://www.health.harvard.edu/blog/ketogenic-diet-is-the-ultimate-low-carb-diet-good-for-you-2017072712089

Paoli, A. (2014, February 19). *Ketogenic Diet for Obesity: Friend or Foe?* Retrieved from US National Library of Medicine National Institutes of Health: https://www.ncbi.nlm.nih.gov/pmc/articles/PMC3945587/#B13-ijerph-11-02092

Other Cookbooks by Brendan Fawn

VEG RECIPES

https://www.amazon.com/dp/B07C6MZF8

KETO FAT BOMBS

https://www.amazon.com/dp/B07DZJJWP6

Keto Fat Bombs: 30 Sweet Fat Bomb Recipes and Keto Desserts

https://amzn.to/2tMUzt7

Keto Fat Bombs: 30 Chocolate Fat Bomb Recipes and Keto Fat Bombs Snacks

https://www.amazon.com/dp/B07DZJJWP6

Made in the USA
San Bernardino, CA
22 February 2019